# Desert Snakes

## by James W. Cornett

Cover photograph:
Gopher Snake, *Pituophis catenifer,*
Red Rock Canyon
National Scenic Area, Nevada.

Back cover photograph:
Glossy Snake, *Arizona elegans,*
Sonoran Desert, California.

Title page photograph:
Desert Striped Whipsnake, *Masticophis taeniatus*
Great Basin Desert National Park, Nevada.

Contents page (page 3) photograph:
Gopher Snake, *Pituophis catenifer*,
Red Rock Canyon
National Scenic Area, Nevada.

Introduction page (page 5) photograph:
Lyre Snake, *Trimorphodon biscutatus,*
Saguaro National Park, Arizona.

Page 72 (back page) photograph:
Sidewinder track
Anza-Borrego Desert State Park, California.

Photographs by the author.

Published by

**nature trails press**

P.O. Box 846
Palm Springs, California 92263
Telephone (760) 320-2664
Fax (760) 320-6182

International Standard Book Number (ISBN): 0-937794-34-1

# Contents

## Dangerous Snakes

# Introduction

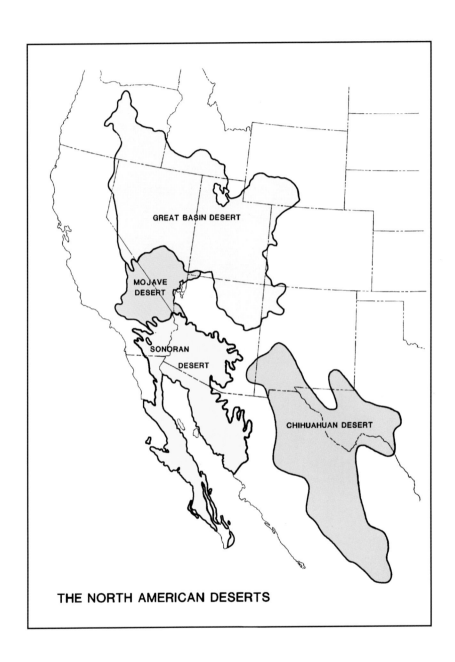

GREAT BASIN DESERT

MOJAVE
DESERT

SONORAN

DESERT

CHIHUAHUAN DESERT

THE NORTH AMERICAN DESERTS

To many people, deserts are synonymous with snakes. The popular thinking goes something like this: "Deserts are hot and snakes thrive in the heat." This belief is partially correct. Snakes and other reptiles are coldblooded and require external sources of heat (the sun, warm air, or warm earth) to heat their bodies, increase metabolic rate, and enable activity. Our desert regions are warm during much of the year and so from that perspective favor the existence of snakes.

The coldbloodedness of reptiles, or exothermy as it is more properly termed, stands in dramatic contrast to the warmbloodedness of birds and mammals. These latter groups create their own internal heat by rapidly burning (oxidizing) food. This normally requires constant, or at least daily, feeding and enables mammals, as well as birds, to be active even in cold weather.

In a desert environment, however, food is not always available. Deserts are notorious for unreliable precipitation resulting in unpredictable food resources. Warm-blooded animals can be at a distinct disadvantage when food is not available. With high metabolic rates, mammals and birds may succumb to starvation during periods of prolonged drought.

By contrast, snakes and other reptiles take refuge in the cool confines of a burrow during times of food scarcity. In such surroundings their metabolic rates drop and they can exist weeks or even months without food or water. This is one reason why snakes and other reptiles are so well represented in hot desert regions.

There is another phenomenon that explains the diversity of snakes in the desert Southwest. It involves the remarkable variety of landscapes. The Southwest is not a vast flatland extending from horizon to horizon. Rather, it is a collage of environments made up of mountains, dunes, boulder fields, canyons, washes, cactus forests and even seashores. All other things being equal, such a complex desert will have more species than a simple flatland. This is a result of the greater number of opportunities for snakes and other animals to exploit the food, shelter, or thermal resources in a complex environment. Each opportunity supports a different species. Garter and lyre snakes, for example, are habitat specialists and their occurrence is allowed by the presence of particular kinds of environments.

A final reason for snake diversity in the American deserts is the warm nights in late spring, summer and early fall. Warm nights allow snakes to maintain a relatively high metabolic rate even after the sun has set. They can be active in darkness and thus better able to surprise many types of prey, particularly lizards most of which become lethargic at night. (Snakes are also more likely to elude their own predators at night.) The expanded period in which hunting takes place increases both the abundance and diversity of snakes. This is the principle reason that the relatively cool Great Basin Desert supports just nine snake species, that the warmer Mojave Desert harbors twenty species and that the even warmer Sonoran Desert supports twenty-nine species, not counting several additional varieties found in the Sonoran Desert of Mexico.

The snake species, or groups of closely related species, that occur in the Mojave and Sonoran deserts are included within this book. It includes most, but not all, of the species living in the Great Basin and Chihuahuan deserts. The maps show the approximate range of each species, or the accumulated ranges of all the species in a single genus. Some essentially mountain, prairie, or coastal species may be found along desert edges. These species are not included within this publication.

The order in which individual snake species appear in this book is based upon the relationships and length of time individual species or groups of species are thought to have been in existence (a concept referred to as phylogeny). The ancestry of the western blind snake, for example, is very old compared with that of rattlesnakes. Thus the western blind snake is the first species to be described in the text and the rattlesnakes appear at the end of the book. Paleontologists and taxonomists examine fossils and compare the anatomy of living species to determine which species represent ancient lineages and which evolved more recently.

Harmless species accounts are denoted by green page numbers; dangerous species are identified by red page numbers. Contrary to the notions of uninformed people, the majority of desert snakes are harmless, not dangerous. Even with regard to the dangerous species none of them can be considered deadly. The overwhelming majority of venomous snake bite victims recover, they don't die. Death by snake bite in the United States is an extraordinarily rare event amounting to less than ten persons per year.

Since most snakes are quite harmless, with only a relatively few that are dangerous (and none deadly), there is no justification for killing a snake on sight. For those who are fearful of snakes, it is best to simply walk away from any serpent encountered. It is hoped, of course, that publications like this will lessen peoples' fear of snakes and encourage them to consider both the beauty and remarkable adaptations of these strange, legless creatures.

Most of the persons who read this book are quite fascinated by snakes and revel in the seeming abundance and diversity of these creatures. They seek more information and new perspectives. Many aficionados even keep one or more serpents as pets. The collecting of large numbers of wild snakes for personal collections, however, should be discouraged. As carnivores, snakes are near the top of the food pyramid and their numbers are necessarily few in comparison with the plant or insect eating animals on which they feed. In many regions snake populations have been seriously depleted by overzealous collectors. Using the technique of driving down little-traveled roadways on warm nights, a dozen or more snakes may be picked up in a single hour. No snake population can survive such collection pressure for long.

There is an alternative for snake fanciers. Many commercial reptile breeders sell the most sought-after species for a fraction of what it would cost to secure the same individuals in the wild. Each year, the number of available species increases. These enterprises have and will continue to take tremendous collection pressure off wild populations while at the same time promoting a healthy interest in reptiles. The simplest way to find and contact reptile breeders is via the internet.

The common and scientific names used in this book are taken from the most authoritative and readily available text on reptiles of the western United States, Robert C. Stebbins' *A Field Guide to Western Reptiles and Amphibians*. This book is highly recommended for those seeking additional information regarding all desert reptiles. (Readers should be aware that the common and scientific names of some snake species have changed since 1985 when Stebbins' guide was last published. Unfortunately, these changes are widely scattered in the scientific literature and not readily accessible to laypersons. Therefore Stebbins' names are, in most instances, used in this publication.)

Although I have relied heavily upon my own experience and research involving desert snakes, I have also utilized the knowledge and research of others. The efforts of those individuals are reflected in the references section at the end of this book. Herpetologists Mark Fisher and Lee Grismer graciously reviewed the manuscript for technical accuracy. Clifford Neff and my wife, Terry Cornett, reviewed the manuscript for grammatical errors and made suggestions for improving the clarity of my writing. Sincere appreciation is extended to all of these individuals.

*Sonoran Desert bajada in Saguaro National Park, Arizona.*
*Habitat of the Saddled Leaf-nosed Snake, Long-nosed Snake, and Western Coral Snake.*

# Harmless Snakes

*Western Blind Snake*
*Sonoran Desert, southeastern California.*

# Blind Snakes
## Genus *Leptotyphlops*

The pink coloration, slender body, and short length give this snake the appearance of an earthworm. The blind snake, however, possesses a skeleton, brain, and lungs, features absent in all worms. The girth of the blind snake is half that of a pencil and rarely does one exceed a foot in length. Two species exist in the American deserts: the western blind snake, *Leptotyphlops humilis* of the Mojave, Sonoran and southern Great Basin deserts; and the texas blind snake, *L. dulcis*, of the Chihuahuan Desert.

As the common name indicates, blind snakes have no functional eyes. Opaque scales cover what remains of eye structures or *vestigial* eyes and, at best, an individual snake may be able to distinguish light from dark but nothing else. Long ago, the ancestors of blind snakes possessed functional eyes but the need for these were lost when a subterranean lifestyle was adopted. (Scientists use the term *fossorial* to refer to living underground.) Eyes are of no value and can even be a hindrance when moving through soil. The production of eyes and other features of animals are energetically expensive and, through time and evolution, can be expected to diminish in size and functionality when they no longer promote a species' survival.

Although the blind snake's small size and erratic movements above ground make it seem rather helpless, it is not without defenses and can employ three strategies to deal with threats. When picked up it discharges a smelly fluid from the anus that functions to make it unappetizing to predators. Humans can detect the smell from several feet and so one would assume it is a particularly effective deterrent against small predators. A blind snake also possesses a spine at the end of its tail that is used as a tiny dagger to prick enemies. (If a blind snake is picked up the push of the spine can be felt though it cannot penetrate the relatively thick skin of humans.) Of course rapidly burrowing into the soil is the best escape strategy.

Blind snakes feed almost exclusively on ants, termites, and the eggs and larvae of these insects. These are captured in underground tunnels and corridors. Like other snakes they often protrude their tongue to smell the location of prey.

Blind snakes are widespread in desert regions wherever loose pockets of soil exist. They are rarely seen, however, due to their fossorial life style. Specimens are occasionally found in late spring as they cross paved roads or in pit traps set up as part of research projects. It is presumed that they are searching for mates when found on the surface in May and June. More distance can be covered above ground than below it and thus blind snakes increase their chances of finding a partner by surfacing. Several weeks after copulation, females lay from two to six eggs.

*Rosy Boa*
*Anza-Borrego Desert State Park, California*

# Rosy Boa
*Lichanura trivirgata*

One need not travel to the American tropics to encounter a boa. Though considerably smaller than its close relative the boa constrictor, the rosy boa possesses all the attributes of snakes in the family referred to as Boidae. Boas are best known for encircling prey with coils of their body and squeezing their victims to death. Although snakes in some other families also possess this ability, the powerful, heavy-bodied boas are masters of the technique and able to subdue rodents larger and more quickly than similar-lengthed gopher or kingsnakes. Unlike their huge relatives, a very large rosy boa reaches a maximum length of just under four feet.

The primitive nature of a boa is revealed by the presence of rudimentary hind limbs just in front of the anal opening on the snake's underside. These hind limbs appear as two, single, tiny claws used by the male to stroke a female during copulation. Dissection of a dead boa reveals a vestigial pelvic girdle as well. Both these features are evidence that the ancestors of boas and other snakes were creatures with legs that walked, rather than crawled.

The rosy boa is restricted in its distribution to rocky hillsides and canyons where its superb climbing ability gives it a competitive advantage over other, similar-sized constricting snakes. The species occupies most desert mountain ranges from Hanaupah Canyon in the Panamint Mountains of Death Valley National Park, south through Anza-Borrego Desert State Park, California, and west to Organ Pipe Cactus National Monument in Arizona.

Although its vertical pupils might suggest a strictly nocturnal activity regime, rosy boas are sometimes found during the day in April and May. Most encounters are at night, however, when rosy boas are seen on roadways. Rosy boas, as well as many other desert snakes, are frequently encountered in spring when they emerge on the surface in search of mates. Unlike most of our desert snakes, rosy boas give birth to their young alive. Technically speaking, boas are ovoviviparous which means that eggs without shells hatch in the mother's body and the young are born as small, fully-formed boas.

The rosy boa is highly variable in color. Specimens from the western edge of the desert in California have three irregular, deep purple stripes. In Organ Pipe Cactus National Monument rosy boas are light gray with chocolate brown stripes.

In addition to rodents, the rosy boa preys upon birds and young cottontail rabbits.

*Ringneck Snake from the Providence Mountains,*
*Mojave National Preserve, California. Note, this individual lacks the characteristic neck ring.*

# Ringneck Snake

*Diadophis punctatus*

The orange band around its neck accounts for the common name of the ringneck snake. Many isolated desert populations lack the neck ring entirely, however, making identification difficult. Fortunately, the underside of the tail is bright red and the snake both coils and turns its tail upward when it is threatened. This behavior and the bright color help distinguish the ringneck snake from other desert serpents. The maximum recorded length for a ringneck is thirty inches but most individuals are seldom even twenty inches long.

Defense is the function of the coiled-tail display and no doubt startles a predator that may hesitate long enough for a ringneck to escape. It might also direct an attack at the tail where musk glands, capable of discharging a foul-smelling fluid, are located. Should the tail display fail, ringnecks are known to feign death. These last two strategies function to make the snake unappetizing, or at least uninteresting, as prey. As a last resort, ringnecks may also bite.

There is some evidence suggesting that ringneck snakes possess a mild venom. (One observer reported a burning sensation after he was bitten.) They have enlarged rear teeth in the back of their jaws and there are scattered accounts of venom-like effects in prey. Ringnecks feed on a wide assortment of animals including skinks and other small lizards, treefrogs, salamanders, young gopher and garter snakes, and possibly insects. Struggling prey may be partially constricted with loops of the ringneck's body.

Breeding commences in spring after adults emerge from hibernation. Ringneck eggs are laid in an advanced stage of development and hatch in about half the time of other oviparous species, from five to six weeks as compared with up to twelve weeks.

Of all the snake species known to occur in the Southwest deserts, the ringneck is encountered least often. It is really a snake of cooler, moister environments and is abundant in mountains, coastal hills, and chaparral. Nevertheless, it does occur in many desert ranges. All four of the author's desert observations have occurred in the spring months and include an individual found crawling amongst saguaro cacti at the base of the Kofa Mountains in western Arizona, one found crossing a trail near Mitchell's Caverns in the Providence Mountains of the Mojave National Preserve, a third swimming in a palm-oasis pond at the base of the Peninsular Ranges, and a fourth captured in a pit trap in the pinyon-juniper woodland of the Santa Rosa Mountains.

*Spotted Leaf-nosed Snake*
*Joshua Tree National Park, California*

# Spotted Leaf-nosed Snake
*Phyllorhynchus decurtatus*

The spotted leaf-nosed snake is the quintessential desert serpent. It is found in the driest regions of the southwest deserts including the Colorado Desert subdivision of the Sonoran Desert, and the Mojave Desert's Death Valley. Additionally, unlike most desert snakes that are occasionally encountered during daylight hours, it is strictly nocturnal. Finally, the majority of desert snake species have distributions that extend into other, non-desert environments. The range of the leafnosed, however, is wholly confined to desert.

For many decades the spotted leaf-nosed snake was thought to be the rarest of all desert reptiles. Only a handful had made their way into museum collections. Then, with the construction of paved roadways in desert areas in the 1930s, Lawrence Klauber of the San Diego Zoo discovered that large numbers of snakes could be found on road surfaces at night, particularly on warm spring evenings. The snakes were presumably crawling about in search of mates and lingered on the pavement, perhaps attracted by the heat that had built up during the day. Klauber found many kinds of reptiles but discovered that leaf-nosed snakes were particularly easy to collect. Before long, what was once considered to be the desert's rarest was found to be its most common snake.

The common name of this species is derived from the unusual scale on its nose (called the rostral scale). It is large, triangular, and quite noticeable even though leaf-nosed snakes are only twelve to twenty inches in length. Herpetologists generally agree that the scale is helpful in burrowing into the soil. In the wild their burrowing proclivities are thought to center around obtaining food, particularly digging for lizard eggs and perhaps even the eggs of other snakes. Examination of leaf-nosed snake stomachs have yielded lizard eggs on several occasions. Apparently, leaf-noses are the only snake species in the southwest deserts whose diet consists primarily of lizard eggs. Other prey discovered in leaf-nosed snake stomachs includes lizards, lizard tails, and insects.

Very little is known regarding the reproductive habits of leaf-nosed snakes. Presumably mating takes place in spring since this is the time when leaf-noses are most active. Females are oviparous (egg-laying) and produce from two to five eggs per clutch. Eggs are probably laid in abandoned rodent burrows and its is likely that some attempt is made to cover them with dirt as protection from desiccation and predators. Information gleaned from captured females carrying eggs indicates that egg-laying occurs in June and July with one clutch laid per year.

*Saddled Leaf-nosed Snake*
*Organ Pipe Cactus National Monument, Arizona*

# Saddled Leaf-nosed Snake

*Phyllorhynchus browni*

The saddled leaf-nosed snake is one of the desert's most beautiful reptiles. The unusual shades of pink and brown are combined in patterns that are striking to humans yet make for excellent camouflage on the relatively dark, rhyolitic soils found throughout much of this species' range.

An interesting feature of leaf-nosed biology is the similar habits and ranges of the saddled and spotted leaf-nosed snakes. Though they differ noticeably in pattern and moderately in color, everything else about the two species appears the same. They reach the same lengths, feed on lizards and their eggs, and have overlapping ranges in the eastern Sonoran Desert of Arizona. Biologists generally agree that no two species can occupy the same niche. That is to say that no two species can eat the same food, live in the same place, and be active at the same time. If this competitive exclusion principle, as it is called, is valid, how can these two closely related species coexist? A close examination of the habits of the two species suggests that there are differences in their lifestyles.

In the experience of most field herpetologists, the spotted leaf-nosed snake is usually active in spring whereas the saddle leaf-nosed snake is more often encountered in summer after the arrival of the monsoon rains in southern Arizona. With regard to habitat preference the saddled leaf-nose is found in upland desert regions—on alluvial fans and desert hills—whereas the spotted leaf-nose is more of a flatland snake occupying dryer basin floors. In short, it appears that these two species coexist in the same general region by being active at different times of year and existing in different habitats.

One might ask why the saddle leaf-nosed snake does not occupy the Colorado Desert of California. It is interesting to note that the range of this species falls entirely within the distribution of the saguaro cactus, a plant that requires summer rain—rain that is generally absent in the Colorado Desert. The greater productivity of the eastern Sonoran Desert, with both winter and summer rainfall, results in a greater abundance and diversity of lizards, the preferred food of the leaf-noses. The increased availability of food allows niches to be narrowed, thus accommodating two leaf-nosed species rather than just one. In the dryer Colorado Desert of California, the niche must be expanded leaving room for only one species. As one might expect, the spotted leaf-nosed occupies all habitats in the Colorado Desert.

It should come as no surprise that a small snake lacking venom and constricting ability has many predators. Chief among these are other snakes, particularly the much larger long-nosed snake that occupies all the habitat and ranges of the leaf-noses and has the capacity to constrict prey.

*Coachwhip*
*Joshua Tree National Park, California*

# Coachwhip

*Masticophis flagellum*

The coachwhip is an extremely active, fast-moving, diurnal reptile with a pugnacious disposition. When captured, it bites repeatedly causing painful, though minor, wounds as a result of it pulling away before the teeth are free.

Countless times I have come upon a coachwhip only to have it disappear into a burrow or dense shrub. When a tree is present it escapes by climbing into the crown. The coachwhip appears to move very rapidly but the top speed is less than five miles per hour, not even a quarter that of a human sprinter. The slender, four to six-foot-long body, and multiple patterns aid in the illusion of speed. The observer concentrates on one pattern and the image is impressed upon the retina. After the snake is gone, the eye continues to record the pattern. (The effect is like looking at a bright object and seeing the object after closing your eyes.) Such a phenomenon can confuse a roadrunner or hawk, long enough for the coachwhip to escape.

The coachwhip forages primarily by sight. It scouts out the terrain by lifting its head several inches off the ground. Should prey be seen, it moves the head from side to side, possibly as an aid in depth perception. Prey movement attracts a coachwhip closer until a sudden rush catches the victim unaware. Prey is swallowed alive though large victims are simultaneously held to the ground with a loop of the body.

The coachwhip is fond of nestling birds and I once had the opportunity of watching the hunting behavior used for this purpose. I had set up my camping gear near a palo verde tree, sat down, and began reading. I was motionless for an hour when I glanced up and saw a large coachwhip approach the trunk of my tree. It slithered into the branches and seemed to know exactly where it was going, heading straight for the nest of a house finch. The nest was empty and, upon determining this, the snake moved through the tree to a verdin's nest. It, too, was empty. I watched the snake crawl to the ground and head for another palo verde some distance away.

In addition to nestling birds, coachwhips are known to feed upon many other animals including small rodents, lizards and other snake species including small rattlers. Presumably they are immune to rattlesnake venom, as is the kingsnake. Some insects are also consumed, especially sphinx moth caterpillars.

Mating occurs in April and the female deposits up to sixteen eggs a few weeks thereafter. Within eleven weeks the eggs hatch giving forth pencil-girthed young about fifteen inches in length. The lifespan of coachwhips in the wild is unknown but one captive individual lived sixteen years.

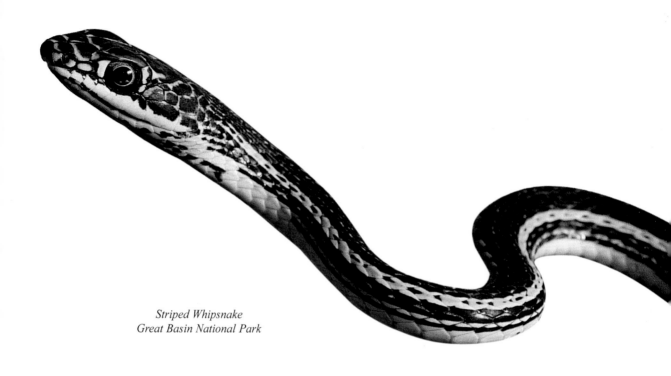

*Striped Whipsnake*
*Great Basin National Park*

# Striped Whipsnake
## *Masticophis taeniatus*

The striped whipsnake is a close relative of the coachwhip with similar habits and behavior. It is strictly diurnal and actively forages over the ground in search of almost any animal that is alive and can be subdued. This includes the larvae and adults of large insects, lizards, other snakes, birds, eggs, and small mammals such as pocket and white-footed mice.

The first striped whipsnake I encountered alive was in Great Basin National Park. I was driving up the grade that takes visitors to the park visitor center when I spotted a snake's head raised six inches above the road shoulder. I quickly turned the car around and came to rest on the shoulder opposite the snake. It was an impressive specimen, nearly five feet in length and hunting with its head elevated well off the ground. I got out of the car and as I approached, the snake turned and disappeared into the sagebrush. A second encounter occurred at the bottom of the Grand Canyon. Friends and I were rafting down the Colorado River and had stopped in the afternoon to set up camp. No sooner had I laid down on my sleeping bag than a striped whipsnake raced under my mattress. I dared not raise up for fear of crushing the serpent. It was at least five minutes before it emerged and then climbed high into the tamarisk shrub.

Although the striped whipsnake has an extensive and contiguous distribution stretching from Washington to Texas, there are many isolated populations detached from the principle range. For example, a population occurs in the Kofa Mountains of western Arizona but does not extend into the surrounding desert lowlands. This is expected since the species is normally found in cooler and higher upland regions. The Kofa Mountains offers this kind of desert habitat and the surrounding lowlands do not. Thus the striped whipsnakes in the Kofas may be thought of as trapped like a marooned human on an oceanic island. During the Pleistocene Epoch, that ended 10,000 years ago, conditions were cooler with more precipitation. At that time the lowlands were hospitable to the striped whipsnake and it moved easily between mountain ranges. With the desertification of the Southwest at the close of the Pleistocene, striped whipsnakes were forced into higher elevations and became trapped in mountain refugia. The precise environmental factor, or factors, that today prevents them from leaving their desert mountain retreats is unclear. Some herpetologists suspect, however, that the larger, more aggressive coachwhip occupying the lowlands surrounding these mountains plays a role in the whipsnake's isolation.

A related species, the Sonoran whipsnake (*Masticophis bilineatus*), occurs in the Sonoran Desert of southcentral Arizona. The females of both species lay up to twelve eggs in early summer.

# Western Patch-nosed Snake

*Salvadora hexalepis*

The lifestyle and anatomy of this species is similar to that of the whipsnakes. It is slender, fast moving and active during daylight hours. It also has a pugnacious disposition, striking repeatedly when cornered or threatened. The patchnose has a similar diet to that of the whipsnakes feeding on lizards, smaller snakes, and rodents. Like the whipsnakes it is found in most of the desert Southwest and occupies many habitat types.

The patch-nosed snake, however, is decidedly smaller than any whipsnake. With a maximum length of just under four feet it weighs less than half the average-sized whipsnake. The question arises as to how the patch-nosed survives in the face of competition from much larger snakes that live in the same area, are active at the same time, and eat the same food. Consider, too, that whipsnakes readily devour patch-nosed snakes when they chance upon them.

It may very well be that whipsnakes are presently displacing patch-nosed snakes throughout much of the southwestern desert areas. The western patch-nosed snake is uncommon, almost rare. I usually encounter only one or two individuals each year compared with more than two dozen coachwhips. Could it be that a few thousand years from now the patch-nose will be extinct, replaced entirely by a species of whipsnake? The smaller size of the patch-nose, however, and its better camouflage, may be more likely explanations for what seems to be fewer numbers. A reddish or blackish five-foot-long coachwhip is easy to spot. A two-and-one-half foot tan-colored patch-nosed snake can be easily overlooked.

There are some subtle differences in habits that may allow patch-nosed snakes to coexist with whipsnakes and negate the displacement hypothesis. First, patch-nosed snakes are active with lower body temperatures than are whipsnakes. My field notes indicate that they are active earlier in the morning and later in the afternoon. (I even have one record of an adult patch-nosed snake crossing the highway at night.). This could mean that whipsnakes and patch-noses are not hunting at the same time. Patch-nosed snakes also use their greatly enlarged nose scale to dig up reptile eggs, a food apparently ignored by whipsnakes. Finally, patch-nosed snakes are known to use constriction to subdue prey enabling them to consume larger prey than can young, similar-sized whipsnakes.

Mating takes place in spring with female patch-nosed snakes laying from four to ten eggs in late spring or early summer. Eggs are thought to be deposited in abandoned rodent burrows.

*Western patch-nosed snake*
*Mojave National Preserve, California*

*Glossy Snake*
*Anza-Borrego Desert State Park, California*

# Glossy Snake
*Arizona elegans*

The glossy snake is a common species with a broad distribution that includes the Sonoran, Mojave, Chihuahuan and southern Great Basin deserts. It occupies a variety of habitats from the margins of dunes to the upper reaches of alluvial fans. It is only rare on rocky hillsides and in desert mountains.

Along with the leaf-nosed and long-nosed snakes, the glossy snake is one of the most frequently encountered reptiles when *night-driving* down highways. During one three-hour period in the eastern Mojave Desert, I counted eleven glossy snakes but just one spotted leaf-nose snake and one long-nosed snake.

The common name glossy snake comes from the very smooth, shiny scales that reflect even the faintest light. These smooth scales enable the glossy to burrow easily into any loose pocket of soil that it encounters. This includes the dirt plugs that many lizards place at the entrance to their burrows to protect them from nocturnal predators. Using its tongue to pick up a scent trail, the glossy snake hunts for an occupied burrow. When it discovers one, it forces its snout through the plug and traps the lizard in the burrow. (Lizards, typically, have only a single entrance to their nighttime retreat.)

While lizards are the dietary mainstay of glossy snakes, many other animals can become prey. Small rodents such as pocket and white-footed mice top this secondary list, with large individuals also taking kangaroo rats. Snakes, particularly leaf-nosed snakes, have been recorded as food. Like the closely related gopher snake, the glossy is a powerful constrictor. Tight coils are placed around a victim's body keeping the lungs from expanding. Death results from suffocation.

The glossy's fondness for lizards may occasionally lead to its demise. One specimen was found dead, killed by the sharp scales of a horned lizard. The snake had attempted to swallow the lizard but as it passed through the esophagus the head spines of the lizard punctured the snake's throat. One would assume that glossy snakes with a taste for horned lizards seldom live long enough to pass on such an appetite to the next generation.

In the southwestern United States the glossy snake is considered a medium-sized serpent. Most adult individuals encountered are around three feet in length with a maximum recorded length of nearly six feet. As is true of most of our desert snakes, mating is a springtime event with females laying up to twenty-three eggs in early summer.

*Gopher Snake*
*Salton Sea State Recreation Area, California*

# Gopher Snake

*Pituophis catenifer*

The gopher snake is one of the most conspicuous and widespread snake species in the American deserts. Its size can be impressive. Adults typically exceed four feet in length and several individuals have been found that reached seven feet. The large size, together with an impressive defensive display involving coiling, striking, hissing and tail rattling, can make for an unforgettable first encounter. Gopher snakes are unique among desert snakes in that they are capable of making a loud and prolonged hiss when alarmed. The sound is produced by forcing air through the trachea, made unusually narrow because of the presence of a glottal keel, a structure unique to snakes in the genus *Pituophis*.

To the uninitiated, the gopher snake's large-blotched pattern, inhaling of air to expand its body, and habit of flattening the head during defensive displays suggest a rattlesnake. Should the snake be coiled in dry leaves or grass the vibrating tail may even produce a noise that sounds like a rattle. The entire repertoire makes for an intimidating spectacle that is obviously an effective deterrent against enemies. Apparently many enemies mistake gopher snakes for rattlesnakes and leave them alone.

The gopher snake feeds upon rodents including kangaroo rats, woodrats, ground squirrels, gophers (their namesake), pocket mice and white-footed mice. Exceptions to this standard fare include the consuming of lizards particularly by young gopher snakes, and cottontail rabbits by very large individuals. Birds are also eaten. On several occasions I have encountered these snakes in Joshua trees in the Mojave Desert and palo verde trees in the Sonoran Desert. Presumably they climbed the trees in search of nests with eggs or young birds, both of which they are known to eat. Active or struggling prey is killed by constriction. Gopher snakes usually encounter rodents in their burrows and find them primarily through scent tracking. (Snakes smell by constantly flicking their tongue to pick up minute particles that are transferred to "Jacobson's organ" in the roof of the mouth.)

Although desert-inhabiting gopher snakes may be abroad in the morning in early spring, they quickly become nocturnal as the season warms. When found active on the surface in April and May, gopher snakes are usually searching for mates. The olfactory sense is used to locate a mate. The male, by flicking his tongue against the ground, seeks to find and follow a scent trail laid down by a female. Approximately six weeks after mating, the female lays from six to thirty eggs in an abandoned rodent burrow.

*Common Kingsnake*
*Sonoran Desert, California*

# Common Kingsnake
*Lampropeltis getula*

The common kingsnake is an adaptable reptile as much at home on rocky hillsides as on creosote scrub plains or windblown sand hummocks. Localities where moisture is present, such as oases and desert streams, harbor kingsnakes in greatest abundance.

A curious feature of the common kingsnake is its variability in color and pattern. In the Chihuahuan Desert, individuals are black with yellow speckling. In portions of the Sonoran Desert they may be uniformly black. In the desert areas of California and western Arizona kingsnakes are deep brown with white bands. A strikingly different pattern is found in an occasional specimen from Anza-Borrego Desert State Park, in California, where some individuals have a single white stripe running down the back. Banded individuals also live in the Anza-Borrego region and for nearly forty years herpetologists believed the two snakes to be different species. In 1936, however, curators at the San Diego Zoo hatched both striped and banded kingsnakes from the same brood, thus proving the snakes were the same species.

Kingsnakes are known to eat their own kind. This might pose problems during springtime when males and females come together to reproduce. Mating, however, takes precedence over eating and there seems a tendency for these snakes to be less inclined to swallow other kingsnakes during the spring months. Approximately eight weeks following copulation, the female lays four to fourteen pure white eggs. Her involvement ends at that point as kingsnakes, as well as most other reptiles, show no interest in their young after egg laying. Life is hazardous for the newly hatched, ten-inch young, and it is the fortunate kingsnake that reaches maturity. Busy highways, hungry birds of prey, and adult kingsnakes are just some of the perils awaiting them.

The name kingsnake comes from the propensity of this reptile to devour other snakes, including venomous species. It is immune to rattlesnake and coral snake venom enabling it to bite and constrict these snakes as it would any other type of prey. To be sure, a kingsnake prefers not to be bitten since lengthy fangs thrust deep into tissue must be painful and can puncture a heart or lung. But this is usually avoided from the outset by the kingsnake securing a hold on the venomous snake's head.

Other prey includes birds, bird eggs, small rodents, and lizards. Size is probably the most important factor determining what food is taken. Kingsnakes prefer smaller rodents but have been known to swallow fairly large reptiles. There is an authenticated record of a five-foot kingsnake swallowing a six-foot snake. This may seem an impossible feat, but the kingsnake managed it by overlapping the victim into a U-shaped curve in its stomach.

*Long-nosed Snake*
*Saguaro National Park, Arizona*

# Long-nosed Snake

*Rhinocheilus lecontei*

The first reptile I ever found while driving down a desert roadway at night was a long-nosed snake. It was a cool, breezy evening in April. Plant debris and sand were blowing across the road and the air temperature was sixty-six degrees Fahrenheit—conditions not very conducive to snake activity. As I drove slowly down the highway a snake appeared in my headlights. I hurriedly turned the car onto the road shoulder, jumped out and ran over to the snake. It was a long-nosed, nearly three feet in length, with red, yellow, and black scales that glistened in the beam of the flashlight. It was the only snake I saw in three hours of driving that night.

The long-nosed snake is one of the most cold-tolerant desert reptiles. Individuals have been found at night when air temperatures have dropped to sixty-four degrees Fahrenheit. This is also the only snake I have found active in December when all other snakes are hibernating. The tolerance of cool temperatures helps explain the long-nosed snake's extensive range and abundance. Being active on cool nights and during the cooler months lengthens the time in which the long-nose can exploit food resources and search for mates during spring. Ecologically, this translates into a wider distribution and greater density than many other desert snake species.

In the Southwest desert regions, most of the red, black, and yellow snakes are small and often go unnoticed. Examples include the western coral snake and populations of shovel-nosed snakes. The long-nosed snake, reaching a length of three and one-half feet, is easily the largest tricolored serpent, a factor that helps identify adults of this species. It is also the only red, black, and yellow snake living in all four of the North American deserts.

The long-nosed snake is not, however, always tricolored. Some individuals lack the red color and resemble a common kingsnake. Others have black and red saddles with almost no speckling. Scientists sometimes refer to the long-nosed snake, as well as any other animal species with various color forms, as polychromatic. The existence of this phenomenon suggests that intense selection pressure for a particular color or pattern is lacking. Put another way, the specific color or pattern of a long-nosed snake is not particularly important for its survival.

The long-nosed snake is a constrictor and feeds primarily upon reptiles—leaf-nosed snakes are particularly relished. Small rodents, including pocket and white-footed mice, are also eaten.

Breeding begins in March and ends in June making the long-nosed second only to the western patch-nosed snake in length of breeding period. Egg-carrying females are found from June through August. It is believed that some females may lay two clutches in a single season.

*Two-striped Garter Snake*
*Indian Canyons Tribal Park, California*

# Garter Snakes
## Genus *Thamnophis*

So closely are garter snakes associated with aquatic environments that it might seem odd a book on desert snakes would include species in the genus *Thamnophis*. More careful examination, however, reveals that several species of garter snake are terrestrial in their habits. More importantly is the existence of many permanent and seasonal riparian habitats in the North American deserts. These ponds, streams, rivers and lakes support several species of garter snake.

Two great rivers pass through the North American deserts: the Colorado in the Sonoran and the Rio Grande in the Chihuahuan Desert. The lower Colorado supports the checkered garter snake (*T. marcianus*), and the upper course of this same river attracts the black-necked (*T. cyrtopsis*) and western terrestrial (*T. elegans*) garter snakes. The checkered and black-necked garter snakes can also be found along and near the Rio Grande as can the western ribbon snake (*T. proximus*) and common garter snake (*T. sirtalis*). With a maximum length of fifty-two inches, the latter species is the largest garter snake occurring in the desert Southwest.

In the eastern Sonoran and Chihuahuan deserts summer rains create multitudes of temporary ponds that support burgeoning toad populations. Often the black-necked garter snake can be found in these situations in search of amphibians and their tadpoles.

Along the east face of the Peninsular Ranges, at the edge of California's Sonoran Desert, is found the two-striped garter snake (*T. hammondii*). This semiaquatic serpent follows mountain streams down into desert canyons. Here among oasis palms it feeds upon the abundant California treefrog (*Hyla cadaverina*).

Perhaps the most interesting *Thamnophis* population is that of the western terrestrial garter snake surviving in Ash Meadows, Nye County, Nevada. Surrounded by the Mojave Desert, Ash Meadows consists of a series of springs and small streams that support animals that are, in a sense, trapped in a moist island of green.

Garter snakes eat just about anything they can subdue. Frogs, toads, and tadpoles are the typical fare. Like the whipsnakes they cannot constrict and so must swallow prey alive. As a result they must usually consume smaller animals and feed more often.

Unlike a majority of our desert snakes, garter snakes are ovoviviparous—the female's eggs develop fully within her body and the young are born alive. Garter snakes produce more offspring than any other snake within the American Southwest. Broods of a dozen or more are common.

*Ground Snake from the Mojave Desert of California.*

# Ground Snake
## *Sonora semiannulata*

If I were asked to name the rarest snake in the American deserts I might name the ground snake. This species occurs in all four North American Desert subdivisions and a remarkable array of habitats—from sagebrush plains and rocky hillsides to sand hummocks and river bottoms. Yet in more than thirty years of studying desert fauna I have only encountered three individuals. One was found dead on a highway in Death Valley National Park, a second specimen was crossing a road near Randsburg in the Mojave Desert, and a third was found at night on a paved roadway near Tucson, Arizona. Some snakes are considered rare because they have very limited geographical ranges. Within their range they may be common. It is very unusual for such a wide-ranging species, such as the ground snake, to be encountered so infrequently.

At least part of the explanation for the paucity of observations is the snake's size. With a maximum length of just one and a half feet, and a girth no bigger than a pencil, this snake is easily overlooked. Even more important in explaining why this species is so rarely seen relates to its behavior. The ground snake is usually active above ground at night when humans are indoors and asleep. It also spends a great deal of time hiding in rock crevices and burrows and is more reluctant than other snakes to reveal itself. In short, the ground snake may actually be more common then we realize. There is a difference between being rare and being rarely encountered.

The ground snake is unusual in that it comes in a great variety of colors and patterns. It is even more polychromatic than the long-nosed snake. It can have a pattern of dark rings, saddles, a vertebral stripe, or a single neck ring. The ground color may be brown, red, orange, or gray. These patterns and colors can be combined in an array of forms and are usually associated with particular geographic areas. Sometimes, however, banded or striped individuals are all found in the same locality. The net result of this variation is that identification can be difficult. (It is helpful to remember that most individuals have a dark spot on the front of each scale.)

The ground snake feeds on invertebrates including insects and their larvae, spiders, small scorpions and centipedes. There are grooves on the teeth in the rear of the jaw and this suggests that this species may subdue prey with venom (though it is not dangerous to humans). Herpetologists believe that grooves on the teeth of reptiles facilitates the entry of venom into wounds caused by a bite.

The ground snake is oviparous, the female laying up to a half dozen eggs in summer. Males are known to engage in non-lethal combat for mating rights.

*Sonora Shovel-nosed Snake*
*Organ Pipe Cactus National Monument, Arizona*

*Western Shovel-nosed Snake*
*Mojave National Preserve, California*

# Shovel-nosed Snakes
## Genus *Chionactis*

Shovel-nosed snakes are abundant serpents found throughout the Sonoran and Mojave deserts. They are frequently seen on roads at night and often fall into pit traps set out by scientists to sample local fauna.

Two species occupy the deserts of America. The most widespread is the western shovel-nosed snake, *Chionactis occipitalis*. Its range extends from the southern Great Basin Desert of Nevada, south through the entire Mojave Desert and through the Sonoran Desert to Tucson, Arizona. The Sonoran shovel-nosed snake, *Chionactis palarostris*, has a much more restricted range. It is confined to the vicinity of Organ Pipe Cactus National Monument and adjacent Sonora, Mexico. Though shovel-noses burrow effortlessly through the sand of dunes and hummocks they are also found on rocky alluvial fans and coarse-soiled bajadas.

Shovel-nosed snakes can be beautifully marked. In Anza-Borrego Desert State Park eastward, the western shovel-nosed snake is tricolored with a ground color of pale yellow overlain with black saddles or bands separated by orange saddles. Specimens from the Algodones Dunes are particularly brilliant. To the north, in the Mojave Desert, the orange saddles are lost and individuals are bicolored. The Sonoran shovel-nosed snake is the most attractive with wide black and red bands separated by pale yellow.

Both species are excellent burrowers with a number of adaptations for pushing through desert sands. The head is flattened and wedge-shaped which facilitates slipping between soil particles. The upper jaw overlaps the lower jaw to keep sand out of the mouth. Nasal valves aid in keeping particles out of the breathing passages. Finally, the body scales are unusually smooth reducing friction when burrowing beneath the surface.

This attractive, appealing snake includes in its diet a number of venomous and otherwise unappealing creatures. Among the snakes' favorite prey are scorpions which they readily attack. Flailing stingers seem only a minor nuisance and shovel-noses are typically stung at least once as they rapidly swallow the scorpions alive. To the best of my knowledge it makes no matter what kind of scorpion is being eaten as long as it is small enough for a twelve- to seventeen-inch serpent to swallow. Shovel-noses are also known to eat most kinds of spiders, including black widows, as well as venomous centipedes.

Females lay from two to four eggs in early summer, approximately three weeks after mating.

*Banded Sand Snake*
*Saguaro National Park, Arizona*

# Banded Sand Snake

*Chilomeniscus stramineus*

The banded sand snake is a supreme desert burrower. When so inclined, this species can disappear into soft sand within one or two seconds, even faster than the western shovel-nosed snake to which it is closely related.

Adaptations for a burrowing life style are dramatic in this species though a strong magnifying glass is necessary to appreciate many of them. Like the shovel-nosed snakes, the head and snout are wedge-shaped but the neck is thick with no apparent constriction. The body is much stouter as well with a maximum length of just ten inches. These features enable the banded sand snake to push harder through the soil. The scales are extremely smooth giving the snake a lustrous shine and reducing friction even more than is the case with the shovel-nosed snakes. The lower jaw is so deeply countersunk into the upper jaw that the snake appears to have no chin—sand does not enter the mouth of this species. And once again, we find a snake with nasal valves to keep sand out of breathing passages. Interestingly, the eyes of this species are upturned. It has been suggested that such an adaptation may allow the snake to lie in wait for prey with its body hidden under the sand and only its eyes and a small part of its head protruding above ground.

As one might expect, very little is known regarding the habits and behavior of this burrowing snake. Individuals are most often found in natural or man made pit traps which they they fall into but cannot climb out. Occasionally, they are encountered on paved roads at night. Food consists of invertebrates including insects, their eggs and larvae, spiders, scorpions, and centipedes.

Perhaps surprisingly, this snake is not just a species of dunes and hummocks. Unlike the western shovel-nosed snake, it is more often found on the coarser soils of desert flatlands, low hillsides, and washes. In these situations it is typically associated with the soft soil beneath perennial shrubs created by the burrowing of rodents.

The range of the banded sand snake is wholly restricted to the Sonoran Desert in Arizona, Baja California, and Sonora, Mexico. Within this region its range overlaps the range of the shovel-nosed snakes though I have never found both species in the same area. When the banded sand snake is present, the shovel-noses are not. Perhaps the competition between the two species is so great that both cannot occupy the same area at the same time.

What little information is available on reproduction indicates that females lay less than five eggs during the summer months.

*California Black-headed Snake,* Tantilla planiceps
*Santa Rosa-San Jacinto Mountains National Monument*

44

# Black-headed Snakes
Genus *Tantilla*

The black-headed snake is a rarely encountered desert serpent. In thirty-five years of desert travels, I have encountered only six individuals. One had fallen unharmed into a five-gallon pit trap established as part of a research project. Two others were found in late spring crawling across paved roadways at night. Three had been found by maintenance crews around the buildings of the Palm Springs Desert Museum where I work. To explain the presence of the snakes around the museum I should mention that the museum abuts the Sonoran Desert hillsides of the San Jacinto Mountains. The snakes inadvertently crawled out of their normal rocky hillside habitat onto the museum grounds.

There are several reasons why black-headed snakes are rarely encountered by humans. All four desert species in the genus *Tantilla* are small, none exceeding even sixteen inches in length, and with a girth less than that of a pencil. Furthermore, the back and sides of each species are various shades of tan or pale brown that blend in readily with the soil on which they crawl. In short, they are difficult to see. Finally, the snakes are secretive, spending most of their lives in animal burrows, rock crevices, or beneath plant debris. On those rare occasions when they do emerge on the surface it is at night when humans are indoors. It is very likely that black-headed snakes are common; it's just that humans usually overlook them because of their appearance and habits.

The black-headed snake is named for its head that is covered with relatively large, black scales. On close examination the head is also found to be quite flat, at least when compared with most other snakes species. This feature undoubtedly helps the snake wedge into narrow rock crevices and tiny insect burrows.

The black-headed snake feeds primarily on arthropods including tiny millipedes, centipedes, spiders and insects, particularly the larvae of beetles. In captivity these snakes usually languish because they refuse to feed.

Black-headed snakes are most likely to be encountered in the spring when individuals emerge to search for mates. A few weeks after mating females lay from one to three eggs, the small clutch partially reflecting the small size of the snake.

Interestingly, the black-headed snake is thought to be venomous since it possesses enlarged, grooved teeth in the back of its jaws. The grooves presumably facilitate the entry of venom into punctures made by the teeth. Due to its small size and reluctance to bite, the black-headed snake poses no threat to humans.

*Night snakes*
*Joshua Tree National Park, California*

# Night Snake
*Hypsiglena torquata*

The night snake is second only to the gopher snake in having the most extensive distribution in the western United States. It is found throughout all four subdivisions of the North American Desert, wherever stabilized soils and scattered rocks and boulders characterize the landscape.

The range of the night snake is closely aligned with that of the abundant side-blotched lizard, *Uta stansburiana*. This should not be surprising since the lizard is an important food for the night snake. The size match is perfect. A full-grown night snake can be expected to reach sixteen inches and the lizard, not counting the tail, typically reaches just over two inches. That is a large enough meal to sustain a night snake for several weeks.

The distributional success of the night snake can by explained by its utilization of the side-blotched lizard as food. The side-blotched lizard relies on ants as a staple food. Ants, particularly harvester ants, withstand seasonal and long-term drought cycles quite well. The ants consume the abundant seeds dropped on desert soils. Even through long periods of drought many ant colonies survive, thus sustaining the side-blotched lizard, which in turn sustains the night snake. The importance of these kinds of food chains, that sustain a series of animal species during prolonged droughts, cannot be overstated.

Though the side-blotched lizard is the most important prey for the night snake, almost any small or recently hatched lizard species will do. Hatchling night snakes do not appear until late summer, at a time when all species of lizard eggs have hatched including, of course, the side-blotched lizard. This insures that young night snakes have plenty of hatchling lizards on which to feed. Small snakes, including blind snakes, frogs and salamanders are also taken when available.

The night snake has enlarged rear teeth in the back of its upper jaw. These fangs facilitate the entry of a mild venom that can be sufficient to kill lizards. In order to envenomate prey, however, the night snake must work the victim far enough into its jaws so that the rear-mounted fangs can penetrate the skin. (Rear-mounted fangs are not nearly as effective as the hollow, front-mounted fangs of coral and rattlesnakes.)

As its name indicates, the night snake is strictly nocturnal and possesses vertical pupils that open wide in the dark. It is relatively common, but its small size and spotted, brownish coloration make it easy to miss even on paved roads.

Breeding occurs in spring with females laying up to nine eggs in late spring or early summer.

*Desert scrub habitat in Anza-Borrego Desert State Park, California.*
*Habitat of the Common Kingsnake, Coachwhip, and Western Shovel-nosed Snake.*

# Dangerous Snakes

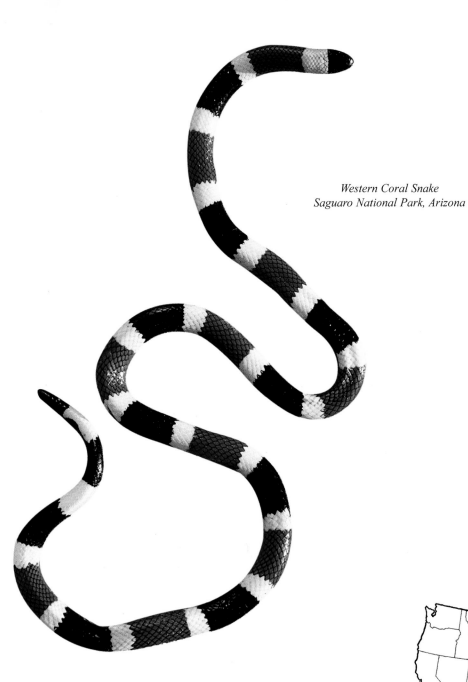

*Western Coral Snake*
*Saguaro National Park, Arizona*

# Western Coral Snake

*Micruroides euryxanthus*

Although it is related to the Indian cobra, and its venom is at least two times more toxic than that of most rattlesnakes, there are no recorded human deaths from the bite of a western coral snake. This fortunate situation is a result of several aspects of the species anatomy and behavior. First, the typical length of an adult coral snake is just sixteen inches and it has a very small head. As a result, the amount of venom it can inject is small. Additionally, the front-mounted fangs do not fold back into the mouth when the jaws are closed, as is the case with rattlesnakes, but rather are fixed and immovable. The fangs are thus necessarily short. Unless a coral snake has an opportunity to chew its fangs into human flesh, it is not likely to penetrate the skin. In addition, the openings through which the venom is injected lie further up on the hollow fangs than is the case with rattlesnakes. This requires that the coral snake imbed its fangs deeper into the victim before venom can be effectively injected.

The venom, however, is potent. It is neurotoxic in its effects and can cause rapid ascending muscular paralysis as well as respiratory paralysis. Herpetologists Charles Shaw and Sheldon Campbell have concisely described the results of three instances where a western coral snake had successfully injected venom into human victims.

> *The symptoms, none of them severe, have been rapid and alike in all three cases. The victims felt pain at the immediate point of the bite, pain which continued from fifteen minutes to a few hours. Some hours after the bite each victim experienced drowsiness, nausea, and weakness. All felt a tingling or prickling sensation, in one instance limited to the finger bitten, but in the other two cases spreading to the hand and wrist. In two of the cases symptoms disappeared within 7 to 24 hours after the bite. In the third and most severe case symptoms persisted for four days—and no wonder for the 22-inch attacking coral snake was the largest ever recorded.*

The habits of the coral snake also contribute to the scarcity of bites. It is a nocturnal species and most likely to be abroad after warm, summer rains—periods when few people are outdoors. The coral snake is also secretive, spending most of its life under rocks or buried in the soil. It is in such places that the western coral snake hunts its prey of small serpents and lizards.

Almost nothing is known of the reproductive habits. Females apparently lay two or three eggs in late summer with an incubation period of approximately two and one-half months. The young are from seven to eight inches in length at hatching.

*Red Diamond Rattlesnake*
*Anza-Borrego Desert State Park, California*

# Red Diamond Rattlesnake

*Crotalus ruber*

The red diamond is one of our largest rattlesnakes, second only to the western diamondback in the southwest deserts. Adults have been known to exceed five feet with a girth comparable to a man's arm. Fortunately, most individuals are surprisingly docile—they rarely strike and often don't even rattle when first encountered.

Drop for drop, the venom of this species is the least toxic of any desert-dwelling species. Its impressive size, however, means that a large quantity of venom can be injected and therefore, mild disposition notwithstanding, it should be considered very dangerous.

The red diamond rattlesnake is widespread in Baja California but barely enters the United States and then only in southern California. Here its range extends slightly into two of California's deserts: the western portion of the Sonoran and southern portion of the Mojave desert.

Naturalists have long puzzled over this species' absence from the vast majority of America's desert lands. It is found in the arid regions of Baja California and shares with the sidewinder the distinction of being one of the most common rattlesnakes in portions of the extreme western Sonoran Desert. In this latter region it occurs in many habitat types from the rocky, lower slopes of mountains out onto flatlands where compacted soils support the growth of scattered creosote bushes and cacti.

Clues as to the limited range of the red diamond in the California deserts may lie in the ranges of two other rattlesnake species. Throughout the Mojave Desert exists a rattler appropriately known as the Mojave rattlesnake, *Crotalus scutulatus*. This is a large rattlesnake that is both more aggressive than the red diamond and possesses a more toxic venom. It also occupies the same sort of habitat—flatlands, hills and lower mountain slopes. The western diamondback rattlesnake, discussed previously, is found throughout most of the Sonoran Desert of California. It, too, is a large rattlesnake both more aggressive and possessing a more toxic venom than the red diamond and is found in the much the same kind of habitat.

The competitive exclusion principle mentioned earlier may explain the present restriction of the red diamond rattlesnake. Recall that no two species can occupy the same place at the same time and eat the same things. Should two similar species ever find themselves occupying the same area, the "more fit" competitor eventually displaces the "less fit" competitor. This may explain why the red diamond presently concedes the Mojave Desert to the Mojave rattlesnake and most of the Sonoran Desert to the western diamondback.

*Speckled Rattlesnake*
*Santa Rosa - San Jacinto Mountains National Monument*

# Speckled Rattlesnake

*Crotalus mitchellii*

The speckled rattlesnake is the species most often encountered by hikers in canyons and mountains of the Mojave and western Sonoran deserts. Unfortunately, this species is difficult to see and is often stepped upon before a hiker is aware of its presence.

Most rattlesnake species possess colors and patterns that help them blend into their surroundings, a phenomenon referred to as camouflage though technically known as concealing coloration. Among rattlesnakes *Crotalus mitchellii* is the best example of this phenomenon. Its subtle speckles and splashes of white, black and earth tones result in it blending into its environment so well that it is incredibly difficult to discern. Even its eye color matches its surroundings.

The reliance of the speckled rattlesnake on concealing coloration is demonstrated by an incident involving an individual of this species and sixteen hikers. The group had been following a trail into a mountain range in California's Anza-Borrego Desert State Park. A boulder, nearly two feet in diameter, was encountered in the middle of the trail. Each hiker was required to step up on the boulder and then continue by stepping back down to the trail. One by one the hikers stepped up and over the boulder. As the last hiker got over the obstacle he turned to admire the view of the valley floor. He also happened to look down and before his eyes was a speckled rattlesnake coiled at the base of the boulder over which sixteen hikers had just stepped. Each hiker had placed his or her boot within twelve inches of the snake and it never moved, rattled or struck. Its camouflage worked! The snake was estimated to be about two and one half feet in length and could have easily reached the ankle of any hiker.

The largest speckled rattlesnake ever found attained a length of nearly six feet, classifying it as a medium-to-large rattlesnake. Though its venom is quite potent this species is not particularly aggressive and generally remains quiet and still even if approached closely. Perhaps this is the reason that bites from *Crotalus mitchellii* are rare and no human deaths have yet been recorded.

Adult speckled rattlesnakes prey upon rodents whereas juveniles feed upon lizards. Very large adults are known to attack small cottontail rabbits. Birds are also taken though obviously complete surprise is required. I once found a speckled rattlesnake curled up alongside a spring in Joshua Tree National Park. A feather protruding from its mouth and a bulge in its torso suggested it had succeeded in capturing a bird that had come in to drink.

Speckled rattlesnakes mate in spring, often during daylight hours, producing up to eleven young in late summer.

*Sidewinder*
*Salton Sea State Recreation Area, California*

# Sidewinder

*Crotalus cerastes*

Just as the rocky mountainside is the domain of the speckled rattlesnake, a flat sandy basin floor is the home of the sidewinder, one of the desert's most unusual rattlesnakes. On open flatlands it is not only a very common reptile but can often be encountered more often than all other snake species combined.

The sidewinder's abundance is appreciated by driving slowly down a paved road on a warm spring evening. Beginning in late March, this species emerges from its underground retreat at dusk in search of mates. If it encounters a paved road still warm from the daytime sun, the snake lingers to absorb the heat. Exposed in this manner the sidewinder is easily seen in automobile headlight beams. I have seen over forty sidewinders in just three hours using this technique!

The name "sidewinder" comes from this reptile's method of locomotion. Most snakes usually move head first in the direction in which their body points. The sidewinder moves perpendicular to the alignment of its body. This odd mode of crawling is accomplished by holding its head and neck flat against the ground then lifting its body and placing it in front of its head. The snake advances as the action is repeated over and over again in a graceful, continuous movement. Although many serpents attempt to sidewind on smooth surfaces, *Crotalus cerastes* does it better and faster than any other North American snake.

The advantage of sidewinding is that it allows the snake to move quickly over very smooth surfaces such as soft sand. Other snakes must shove themselves forward by pushing against irregularities on the surface. This is not as efficient as sidewinding on flat surfaces and particularly on the loose, wind-blown sand that covers much of desert basins.

Another unique feature of the sidewinder is a hornlike scale over each eye. Technically known as *raised supraoculars*, the precise function of these structures had bewildered herpetologists for decades. Several hypotheses had been advanced including shade from the sun and an excess heat radiator. The mystery was resolved when Bayard Brattstrom of California State University at Fullerton showed that the sidewinder folds these scales down over its eyes when buried. Protecting the clear scale over each eye from abrasion is obviously a useful adaptation for a creature living in a environment of windblown sand.

The sidewinder is the smallest desert rattlesnake. The longest specimen ever measured was just under three feet and most adults seldom reach even two feet. The small size coupled with a venom that is of low toxicity explain the paucity of serious envenomations involving this species.

*Black-tailed Rattlesnake*
*Saguaro National Park, Arizona*

# Black-tailed Rattlesnake

*Crotalus molossus*

With a vivid diamond-shaped pattern, contrasting green to yellow ground color, and conspicuous black tail, the black-tailed rattlesnake is striking in appearance. When combined with its sometimes pugnacious disposition, encounters with this species can be memorable events.

The black-tailed rattlesnake is found in a remarkable array of habitats spanning more than nine thousand feet of elevation. In western Arizona it is found on the upper reaches of alluvial fans dominated by saguaro cacti. In the mountains of New Mexico individuals have been found in pine forests over nine thousand feet in elevation. In western Texas, ocotillo-covered limestone canyons harbor this species in abundance. What all of these habitats have in common is rocky or elevated terrain, course soils, and woodrats, a fist-sized rodent that is the black-tail's most frequent prey.

The black-tailed rattlesnake is one of our largest desert rattlers, known to exceed four feet in length. At full adult size these rattlers can prey not just on woodrats, but ground squirrels and cottontail rabbits was well.

Although every desert species of rattlesnake can be found during the daylight hours in early spring, the black-tail is more likely than most to be abroad during the day. No doubt part of this behavior can be explained by the higher, cooler, mountain environments that it so frequently occupies. Another feature of the Black-tail's activity pattern is its propensity to emerge above ground following summer thundershowers, a phenomenon played out in the monsoon season of Arizona, New Mexico, and Texas. One July evening I was driving down an unpaved road in the hills east of Tucson, Arizona. A fifteen-minute downpour (complete with a spectacular lightning show) had soaked the earth leaving many large puddles. Within thirty minutes after the rain had stopped I saw my first black-tail, followed by five more within one hour!

Unlike most desert rattlesnakes that breed in spring, the black-tailed rattlesnake's reproductive season begins with the onset of summer rains in July and August. Females lay down scent trails as they crawl over the ground and males find the trails by smelling them with the aid of their constantly flicking tongue. Courting couples may stay together for several days. Herpetologist Harry Green of Cornell University, discovered that after mating females do not give birth to their young until a full year after insemination. After birth, the three to six young stay with their mother for about a week, until they shed their skin for the first time.

*Tiger Rattlesnake*
*Organ Pipe Cactus National Monument, Arizona*

# Tiger Rattlesnake
*Crotalus tigris*

My first encounter with a tiger rattlesnake occurred years ago on southern Arizona's once-famed Ajo Road, now a highway. I was driving slowly down the paved road, stopping each time I encountered a snake. Careful notes were taken including the species, sex, and length, as well as a hoard of environmental data—time, temperature, wind speed, phase of the moon and so forth.

At 9:32 p.m. on September 7 (I still have my old field notes) a relatively large snake was illuminated in my headlight beams. I immediately pulled off the road, hopped out of the car and ran to the snake. What I saw was a tiger rattlesnake, nearly three feet long and close to the maximum recorded length for the species. Considering its length and girth, it had a surprisingly small head and very large rattle. These features, along with its dark, tiger-like crossbands, instantly revealed its identity. The serpent never struck, coiled, or rattled. Rather, it remained motionless and fully outstretched on the asphalt. I'm sure it was relishing the heat of the road that was retained from the day's sunshine.

Since that time most of the tiger rattlesnakes I have encountered have been abroad in the early morning hours of summer. At such times temperatures are well under ninety degrees Fahrenheit, the normally dry desert air is relatively humid, and long shadows help obscure cryptically colored rattlesnakes from predators. On two such mornings I chanced upon tiger rattlesnakes attempting to enter the large stick nests of woodrats.

The tiger rattlesnake is unusual in that it occurs in only one of North America's deserts, the Sonoran. Even here it is not found everywhere but is confined to the eastern Sonoran Desert of Arizona and adjacent Sonora, Mexico. In this region it is common on upper alluvial fans, hillsides and canyons where saguaro cacti are abundant. Smaller numbers are encountered in the region's mountain ranges where it occurrs in the oak belt up to five thousand feet. With its preference for steep or rocky terrain, the tiger rattlesnake shares a similar ecology with the speckled rattlesnake. In fact, a review of the range maps of the two species suggests that they avoid competition by having separate, though adjoining, ranges.

Whereas most of our desert rattlesnakes are found in spring upon emergence from hibernation, the tiger rattlesnake is dubbed the "fall rattler" because adults are often found abroad in September and October. There is yet to be a satisfactory explanation as to why this is so, but it seems likely that the activity pattern is associated with breeding activities. Like all rattlesnakes, female tigers are live-bearing.

*Western Rattlesnake*
*Joshua Tree National Park, California*

# Western Rattlesnake
## *Crotalus viridis*

The western rattlesnake has the greatest range, is found at the highest altitudes, and occurs in the greatest variety of habitats of any species of rattlesnake in North America. It is found above timberline in the mountains of California, on sagebrush flats in Nevada and at the bottom of Arizona's Grand Canyon.

This is one of the more aggressive rattlesnake species and, like the western diamondback, readily stands its ground when encountered. It is also one of our larger rattlers with specimens commonly over three feet in length. The longest individual on record measured sixty-two inches. Because of its active defense, large size and broad range it is second only to the western diamondback in bites inflicted on humans.

The western rattlesnake is also unique in having evolved the greatest color variation of any U.S. rattler. In mountain forests it can be almost black, on desert flats various shades of brown, and at the bottom of the Grand Canyon hues of orange. The species usually has distinct blotches on the upper surface, however, these blotches remain obscured in the black western rattlers in the mountains of Arizona. In the California deserts individuals range from tan with brown blotches to dark brown with black blotches. In all cases this species has evolved colors that help blend in with the colors of the local environment.

The western rattlesnake is definitely known to den with other snakes. In late fall the snakes from the cold Great Basin Desert seek deep crevices or small caves to escape below-freezing temperatures. Sometimes dozens or even hundreds of individuals use the same retreat. Scientists speculate that this may keep the snakes slightly warmer but more importantly insure that they can easily find a mate upon emergence from hibernation.

The western rattlesnake breeds in spring providing winter rains have been adequate. (In relatively dry years rattlesnakes may not reproduce.) A male generally locates a female by following a scent trail that she leaves as she crawls over the ground. Once located, a male loosely twines his body around the female and inserts one of his two hemipenes into her cloacal opening. As with all snakes, fertilization is internal.

Litter size ranges from six to ten. The young rattlers are fully formed and venomous at birth though they cannot rattle since they have only one rattle segment. A few days after birth they shed their skin, a new segment is added and they are able to make a faint buzzing sound.

*Mojave Rattlesnake*
*Organ Pipe Cactus National Monument, Arizona*

# Mojave Rattlesnake

*Crotalus scutulatus*

The Mojave rattlesnake is notable in having the most toxic venom of any other rattlesnake species. In fact, its venom is approximately eight times more potent than that of the western rattlesnake, the next most virulent serpent found in the American deserts.

The toxicity of the Mojave's venom results from what scientists describe as its "neurotoxic" qualities. These are specific protein components that affect a victim's nervous system, and in serious envenomations can include elevated heart rate as well as cardiopulmonary and respiratory arrest. Death in humans is more likely with this species than any other but is still rare if the victim is treated with antivenin. The venom of most other rattlesnake species affects the tissues rather than the nervous system. These types of venom are termed "hemotoxic" and are much less likely to result in the death of a human victim.

The Mojave rattlesnake is one of the desert's larger species with adults typically exceeding three feet in length with a maximum known length of fifty-one inches. It is also moderately aggressive. These facts, combined with extremely toxic venom, make it the most dangerous snake in the Southwest.

As with each of the eight species of rattlesnake living in the American deserts, the Mojave has adapted to hot, arid conditions by adjusting its activity in accordance with temperature. From late November until the end of February the Mojave is usually hibernating. As temperatures begin to warm in March it emerges from hibernation and is primarily active during daylight hours. With the predictably hot weather in June it becomes nocturnal to avoid temperatures that might otherwise be lethal. Being active at night also has the advantage of reducing water loss through the evaporation of moisture from the tissues of the lungs and other respiratory surfaces. The cooler temperatures and higher relative humidities at night reduce the rate at which water is lost from these surfaces.

Nocturnal activity has other advantages. Under the cover of darkness all species of rattlesnake are less likely to be seen by both prey and predators. With their ability to detect the invisible heat (infrared radiation) given off by warm-blooded animals, they have a tactical advantage over all other animals who rely solely on vision to avoid enemies or find prey.

Unlike many species of rattlesnake that prefer rocky areas, the Mojave is most often found on elevated desert flatlands. It often shares these wide open spaces with the sidewinder and western diamondback rattlesnake.

*Joshua tree woodland in the Mojave Desert, Death Valley National Park, California, habitat of the gopher snake, striped whipsnake, and western rattlesnake.*

# Suggested Reading

Cornett, J. W. 1996. *Rattlesnakes of the California deserts.* Palm Springs Desert Museum, Palm Springs, California.

Cornett, J. W. 1999. *Rattlesnakes: answers to frequently asked questions.* Nature Trails Press, Palm Springs, California.

Ernst, C. H. 1992. *Venomous reptiles of North America.* Smithsonian Institution Press, Washington D.C.

Green, H. W. 1997. *Snakes: the evolution of mystery in nature.* University of California Press, Berkeley, California.

Klauber, L. M. 1972. *Rattlesnakes: their habits, life histories and influence on mankind.* University of California Press, Berkeley, California.

Lowe, C.H., C. R. Schwalbe and T. B. Johnson. 1989. *The venomous reptiles of Arizona.* Arizona Game and Fish Department, Phoenix, Arizona.

Miller, A. H. and R. C. Stebbins. 1964. *The lives of desert animals in Joshua Tree National Monument.* University of California Press, Berkeley, California.

Phillips, S. J. and P. W. Comus (editors). 2000. *A natural history of the Sonoran Desert.* Arizona-Sonora Desert Museum Press, Tucson, Arizona.

Schmidt-Nielsen, K. 1964. *Desert animals: physiological problems of heat and water.* Oxford University Press, Oxford, England.

Shaw, C. E. and S. Campbell. 1974. *Snakes of the American West.* Alfred A. Knophf, Inc., New York, New York.

Stebbins, R. C. 1985. *A field guide to reptiles and amphibians.* Houghton Mifflin Company, Boston, Massachusetts.